TOBY BELFER
Visits Ellis Island

Gloria Teles Pushker

TOBY BELFER
Visits Ellis Island

Illustrated by Judith Hierstein

PELICAN PUBLISHING COMPANY
Gretna 2003

To Mel Tarman for suggesting this story

Sincerest thanks to Anita Bertuccini

The word "Pelican" and the depiction of a pelican are trademarks
of Pelican Publishing Company, Inc., and are registered
in the U.S. Patent and Trademark Office.

Library of Congress Cataloging-in-Publication Data

Pushker, Gloria Teles.
  Toby Belfer visits Ellis Island / Gloria Teles Pushker ; illustrated by Judith
Hierstein.
    p. cm.
Summary: Toby takes a trip to Ellis Island and retraces her family's arrival
in 1904.
  ISBN 1-58980-117-2 (hardcover : alk. paper)
  1. Ellis Island Immigration Station (N.Y. and N.J.)—Juvenile fiction. [1.
Ellis Island Immigration Station (N.Y. and N.J.)—Fiction. 2. Emigration and
immigration—Fiction. 3. Jews—United States—Fiction.] I. Hierstein, Judy,
ill. II. Title.
  PZ7.P97943 Tr 2003
  [E]—dc21

2002156406

Printed in Korea
Published by Pelican Publishing Company, Inc.
1000 Burmaster Street, Gretna, Louisiana 70053

TOBY BELFER VISITS ELLIS ISLAND

Toby Belfer and her grandmother often sat on their porch swing, and Gram would tell her stories about how Toby's great-grandmother's family arrived at Ellis Island. This is their story.

Once upon a time, maybe 1904, in a tiny village in Poland, there lived Zelig, a hat maker, and his wife, Toby. They were Jewish.

Zelig and Toby were peaceful people who loved and protected their seven children—Raezel, Morris, Rachel, Avrum, David, Jennie, and baby Adelaide. They were happy following the laws of the *Torah,* just like everyone else in their village.

One day, something terrible happened!

Soldiers marched in and trampled their gardens and burned down the *synagogue*. They told the villagers they couldn't be Jewish anymore and declared that all the Jewish boys had to become soldiers or go to prison.

The family knew it wasn't safe for them to live there. So guess what they did!

Zelig and Toby took what little money they had saved, packed what food and belongings they could carry, got in their wagon, and quietly left the village with their children.

They traveled by horse and wagon for
miles before they reached the ship
that would bring them to America.

The ship was crammed with other families—from Ireland, Italy, Poland, and Russia—who were also running away in search of freedom.

As they left port, some people on the ship got sick from the constant swaying. A thunderstorm frightened the children and made them cry.

When the sun finally came out, the people came on deck and saw a most beautiful sight—a rainbow and land!

It was Ellis Island. They saw the Statue of Liberty—the symbol of welcome that was a gift to the United States from France. They had reached America at last!

The people, who spoke different languages,
were nervous about learning English, the
language of their new homeland. The children
would now have to go to new schools, make
new friends, and learn
new games.

The passengers took a ferry to the main three-story building. Inside were the luggage check and railroad-ticket office. Upstairs, medical officers looked carefully at the peoples' eyes, checking for diseases others might catch. Otherwise, the sick couldn't stay.

Raezel had pinkeye! Her new best friend, Mary Carmella, from Italy, had a bad cough and fever. The officer put a chalk mark on their sleeves and told them to get out of line and sit on a bench until a doctor could examine them.

The doctor told Mary Carmella she had *tuberculosis,* and she was sent back home.

No wonder Raezel was frightened. She thought she would never see her family again. Of course, she did, and everyone was happy.

On the third floor, the *immigrants* who passed the
medical exams were asked to give their names and
other questions. It was at that time that many people
changed their names. Matel the tailor became Max
Taylor, Raezel became Rosie, and a lady with a green
dress became Mrs. Green.

The legal officials asked where they were planning to live, what kind of work they did, how much money they carried, and how many children they had.

At the personal document station, the inspector asked to see marriage and birth certificates, immunization papers, boat tickets, and passports.

At the education station, the immigrants wrote their names and other words in their languages. An officer tossed beanbags at them and made them walk with a book on their heads to check coordination and balance.

Then, the new Americans stood in long lines at the bank station to exchange their gold and silver for American dollars.

RAILROAD TICKETS TO ALL POINTS

After nearly five hours, everyone was hungry and tired. Zelig's family went to a dining hall. Here, some people saw ice cream for the first time. After eating, they went to the railroad-ticket station for tickets to their final destination.

The thousands, no, millions of people who came through settled all over America. Zelig, Toby, and their family took a train to New Orleans and opened a hat shop. The older children helped in the store after school.

Last year, Toby Belfer and her parents went on vacation to New York. They visited museums, churches, and synagogues.

Most of all, though, Toby Belfer wanted to see the
Statue of Liberty and Ellis Island, where her *ancestors*
landed when they came to America.

Toby and her parents read names of the passengers who came through Ellis Island.

Toby Belfer learned that in 1808 the state of New York bought Ellis Island from Samuel Ellis, a merchant and fisherman, for $10,000. The tour guide said that after 1954 Ellis Island was used as a warehouse. In 1966, Pres. Lyndon Johnson declared Ellis Island part of the Statue of Liberty National Monument. It was reopened and dedicated in 1990.

Today, it is the fabulous museum that Toby Belfer was so anxious to visit. She could hardly wait to tell her Louisiana classmates of her experience.

GLOSSARY

ANCESTOR—Forefather.

IMMIGRANT—One who comes to and settles permanently in a foreign country.

PINKEYE—Conjunctivitis; an infection or allergy that makes the white part of the eye turn red, itch, and feel gritty.

SYNAGOGUE—A place for Jewish worship and religious instruction.

TORAH—A scroll containing the first five books of the Bible.

TUBERCULOSIS—A rare, contagious disease affecting the lungs; less common today than in 1904.

BIBLIOGRAPHY

Http://www.capital.net/~alta/history.htm.

Kavenagh, Katie. *Home Is Where the Family Is*. San Antonio, TX: Raintree Steck Vaughn, 1982.

"Kids Discover Ellis Island," *Kids Discover,* nos. 1054-2868 (May 2002).

Ms Marina Piatkowski's Autobiography. Http://www.capital.net/~alta/meribio.htm.

Richman, Carol. *The Lekachmacher Family*. Seattle, WA: Madrona Publishers, 1976.